WRITE THROUGH IT

a g u i d e d j o u r n a l

Write Through It: A Guided Journal for Teen Girls

This Journal Belongs To:

INTRODUCTION

I noticed how your eyes dropped to the floor when I asked, "Is there anything else?"

Quietness filled the chilly office. Goosebumps ran up my arms but not because of the cold temperature. I sensed that something was going on. The way your mother glanced at you with unspoken questions of her own —she felt it too.

There *was* something else. Actually, there was a lot of 'something else's but could you say it in front of her? You wondered what I would think of you. You thought that maybe something was wrong with you that I wouldn't understand. Sometimes you don't even know what to feel or think. Physically, you feel alright most days, but you have lots of things you're trying to figure out.

These fifteen minutes we share isn't enough time to cover it all. There are just so many things on your mind like...

...*when it's test time, you get so nervous, sweaty palms, heart racing, mind full of everything except the right answers.*

...*how you feel different from everyone else like you don't always fit in.*

...*how you love your family, but sometimes they don't seem to understand what you're going through.*

...*or how the funniest thing happened to you yesterday, but maybe no one will think it's as funny as you did.*

No, we didn't get to talk about any of that, but I want you to know all of it - every single feeling, thought, and idea is worth reflecting on and sharing.

That's what we can do here together. I'll ask you some questions I wish I could have and you can be free to answer honestly.

Here's how you can get the most out of this guided journal.

MONTHLY MOTIVATION

Kick off your month with an affirmation that reminds you of your strengths, growth, and amazingness. Get creative and grab some pencils to add some color to the encouragement. Each affirmation is simple and easy to remember, recite, and rewrite throughout the month.

WEEKLY CHECK-UPS

Change doesn't happen overnight, but when you break things down, it's as easy as 3-2-1! Set small goals, reflect on what matters to you with a journaling prompt, and practice one healthy habit. That's right—you'll focus on one simple thing you can do that's good for your mind, body, soul, and relationships. Pay attention to how you feel as you do it. What makes it hard to do? Did you feel better after completing it? Write down any notes.

I'll also pop in with my *Positive Prescriptions*, where I share encouraging words I tell my patients all the time. Hopefully, these one-liners will get you to think of ways to move from all of those negative thoughts to something more positive - and write about it. Your thoughts are so important, and you have to do your best to manage them every day. When you can't think of anything optimistic or to be happy about, take my words.

Look out for my *Confidence Check-In* too - that's where you can freely write about anything you're not so sure about yet. Write out several questions, a few sentences, or make a short list of compliments all about you! It doesn't matter if everything looks or feels perfect. When I ask 'how are you doing?' I mean it and want an honest answer. I want you to write about how you really feel, not what you think people want to hear or see. Confidence starts with being honest about who you are and what you want. And sometimes you don't know until you write it out.

NOTE-TO-SELF

Use this space for when you need to get things on your heart and mind out and onto paper. Or maybe you could use a quick pep talk—yes, you should tell yourself how awesome you are pretty often. Use these blank pages to write out notes, scribble down reminders, doodle to-do lists, or whatever you need.

I hope these prompts and pages inspire you to be...you. Because you are amazing just as you are. While I may guide you on the journey, this is *your* journal. It's your safe space to share. Don't worry about getting things "right" or spelling everything perfectly. Take a deep breath and let go!

I'm so glad that I have this chance to connect with you and am so proud of you. Your family, teachers, and friends are too! You may not realize it yet but this is such a unique time in your life. As you get older and as your relationships change you need to be able to express yourself to be the healthiest, happiest you.

Being healthy and happy is about taking good care of your mind, body, and soul and journaling is a wonderful practice to do just that.

Journaling is also a simple, easy way to organize your thoughts so that you can be more confident, communicate better, and collect memories. Growing up, I loved writing in my journals and I still have stacks of them. It's nice to go back and re-read what I wrote and see how much I changed over the years. You'll be able to do the same.

No matter how crazy, weird, sad, funny, annoying, exciting, uncertain, happy, hard, simple, or ridiculous life gets, I hope you realize that you are growing and learning. Every day is worthy of your attention.

You may not have all the answers or understand everything that's going on, but you can write through it. And if you can write through it, you can get through it.

I'm cheering you on, one word at a time! Happy Writing!

Love,

Charnetta Colton-Poole, M.D.
aka Dr. CeCe

I am
getting
better
every day.

Write about how this affirmation makes you feel. Or you can simply rewrite it over and over again as a reminder.

THIS WEEK

_____

Dates

3 Things I Have To Do:

❶

❷

❸

2 Things I Am Looking Forward To:

❶

❷

1 Habit I Will Practice:

Color or mark the days you practice this habit. Write notes about how it feels to complete it or any challenges you face.

Walk for 15 minutes every day.

Write a short story about what would happen if you were without internet/wi-fi for a whole day. What's the worst that could happen? What's the best that could happen?

CONFIDENCE CHECK-IN
How are you doing? Write or draw whatever is on your mind or heart.

THIS WEEK

_____

Dates

3 Things I Have To Do This Week:

1

2

3

2 Things I Am Looking Forward To:

1

2

1 Habit I Will Practice:

Color or mark the days you practice this habit. Write notes about how it feels to complete it or any challenges you face.

Try a recipe for a fruit and vegetable smoothie.

| M | T | W | T | F | S | S |

**What is something that's been bothering you a lot lately?
Have you shared it with anyone? Why or Why not?**

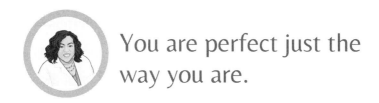

You are perfect just the way you are.

Dates

3 Things I Have To Do:

1

2

3

2 Things I Am Looking Forward To:

1

2

1 Habit I Will Practice:

Color or mark the days you practice this habit. Write notes about how it feels to complete it or any challenges you face.

Dance it out to one of your favorite songs every morning before you start getting ready for school.

Name five people you admire a lot and share why you think they're special.

CONFIDENCE CHECK-IN
How are you doing? Write or draw whatever is on your mind or heart.

THIS WEEK

_____
Dates

3 Things I Have To Do:

1

2

3

2 Things I Am Looking Forward To:

1

2

1 Habit I Will Practice:

Color or mark the days you practice this habit. Write notes about how it feels to complete it or any challenges you face.

Spend two full minutes brushing your teeth and floss twice every day.

| M | T | W | T | F | S | S |

**Think back to one of the happiest moments in your life.
What was the occasion? What made it special?**

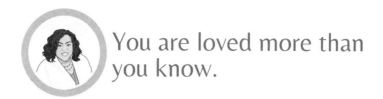

You are loved more than you know.

Write about how this affirmation makes you feel. Or you can simply write it over and over again.

THIS WEEK

_____

Dates

3 Things I Have To Do:

1

2

3

2 Things I Am Looking Forward To:

1

2

1 Habit I Will Practice:

Color or mark the days you practice this habit. Write notes about how it feels to complete it or any challenges you face.

Share with your family members one reason you appreciate each of them.

M T W T F S S

What are your top three favorite things about yourself? What are your top three favorite things about your best friend?

CONFIDENCE CHECK-IN

How are you doing? Write or draw whatever is on your mind or heart.

THIS WEEK

_____
Dates

3 Things I Have To Do:

1

2

3

2 Things I Am Looking Forward To:

1

2

1 Habit I Will Practice:

Color or mark the days you practice this habit. Write notes about how it feels to complete it or any challenges you face.

Take a break from social media (no posting or scrolling) every night between 7pm - bedtime.

| M | T | W | T | F | S | S |

Is there someone you used to like and admire, but you no longer feel the same way? What changed?

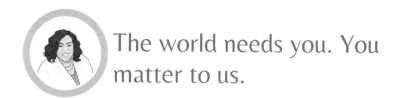

The world needs you. You matter to us.

THIS WEEK

_____

Dates

3 Things I Have To Do:

1

2

3

2 Things I Am Looking Forward To:

1

2

1 Habit I Will Practice:

Color or mark the days you practice this habit. Write notes about how it feels to complete it or any challenges you face.

Find three green-colored fruits or vegetables to eat this week.

Take a moment to remember a really tough school assignment. How did you complete your work? What did you learn about yourself during the experience?

CONFIDENCE CHECK-IN
How are you doing? Write or draw whatever is on your mind or heart.

THIS WEEK

_____
Dates

3 Things I Have To Do:

1

2

3

2 Things I Am Looking Forward To:

1

2

1 Habit I Will Practice:

Color or mark the days you practice this habit. Write notes about how it feels to complete it or any challenges you face.

Commit to not watching TV, scrolling on your phone, or playing video games 30 minutes before you go to bed every night.

Write down your top three songs and why you enjoy them so much.

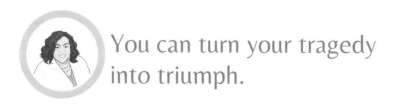

You can turn your tragedy into triumph.

I can always learn new things.

Write about how this affirmation makes you feel. Or you can simply write it over and over again.

THIS WEEK

_____

Dates

3 Things I Have To Do:

1

2

3

2 Things I Am Looking Forward To:

1

2

1 Habit I Will Practice:

Color or mark the days you practice this habit. Write notes about how it feels to complete it or any challenges you face.

Drink a full cup of water first thing when you wake up every day.

Have you ever lied about something? Why did you feel like you had to lie? Did you admit the truth?

CONFIDENCE CHECK-IN

How are you doing? Write or draw whatever is on your mind or heart.

THIS WEEK

_____

Dates

3 Things I Have To Do:

1

2

3

2 Things I Am Looking Forward To:

1

2

1 Habit I Will Practice:

Color or mark the days you practice this habit. Write notes about how it feels to complete it or any challenges you face.

Volunteer to help with cooking dinner.

M | T | W | T | F | S | S

When you think about tomorrow, what's one thing that worries you?
What about next week? Next month? Next year?

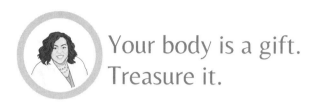

Your body is a gift.
Treasure it.

THIS WEEK

_____

Dates

3 Things I Have To Do:

1

2

3

2 Things I Am Looking Forward To:

1

2

1 Habit I Will Practice:

Color or mark the days you practice this habit. Write notes about how it feels to complete it or any challenges you face.

Text or call a friend or family member you haven't talked to in a while to see how they are doing.

M T W T F S S

What food did you like when you were younger that you hate now? What happened to make you dislike it?

CONFIDENCE CHECK-IN

How are you doing? Write or draw whatever is on your mind or heart.

 **THIS WEEK**

_____

Dates

3 Things I Have To Do:

1

2

3

2 Things I Am Looking Forward To:

1

2

1 Habit I Will Practice:

Color or mark the days you practice this habit. Write notes about how it feels to complete it or any challenges you face.

Share with your favorite teachers, helpful school staff, and leaders why you appreciate them so much.

| M | T | W | T | F | S | S |

Who is your closest friend? Think back to when you first met. Describe how it happened and what made you become good friends.

Always show up for
yourself.

I aim to do
my best.
That's good
enough.

Write about how this affirmation makes you feel. Or
you can simply write it over and over again.

THIS WEEK

_____

Dates

3 Things I Have To Do:

1

2

3

2 Things I Am Looking Forward To:

1

2

1 Habit I Will Practice:

Color or mark the days you practice this habit. Write notes about how it feels to complete it or any challenges you face.

Find two orange-colored fruits or vegetables to eat this week.

| M | T | W | T | F | S | S |

You've just found that when you become an adult you will be granted three wishes. What would you wish for first?

CONFIDENCE CHECK-IN

How are you doing? Write or draw whatever is on your mind or heart.

THIS WEEK

_____

Dates

3 Things I Have To Do:

1

2

3

2 Things I Am Looking Forward To:

1

2

1 Habit I Will Practice:

Color or mark the days you practice this habit. Write notes about how it feels to complete it or any challenges you face.

**Spend an extra 30 minutes studying or reviewing your notes
from school every day.**

| M | T | W | T | F | S | S |

Imagine it's senior year and graduation is right around the corner. Who would you like to spend your last few days of high school with and why?

A good diet now leads to good habits for a lifetime.

THIS WEEK

_____

Dates

3 Things I Have To Do:

1

2

3

2 Things I Am Looking Forward To:

1

2

1 Habit I Will Practice:

Color or mark the days you practice this habit. Write notes about how it feels to complete it or any challenges you face.

Read the nutrition label for everything you eat this week.

M T W T F S S

Think back to last month. What was the funniest thing you saw or heard?

CONFIDENCE CHECK-IN
How are you doing? Write or draw whatever is on your mind or heart.

THIS WEEK

_____
Dates

3 Things I Have To Do:

1

2

3

2 Things I Am Looking Forward To:

1

2

1 Habit I Will Practice:

Color or mark the days you practice this habit. Write notes about how it feels to complete it or any challenges you face.

Listen to a style or genre of music you don't usually like.

M T W T F S S

List out all the questions on your mind right now. Underline questions you can ask someone about and circle the ones that confuse you. Think of someone who may be able to answer and ask them.

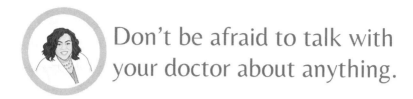

Don't be afraid to talk with your doctor about anything.

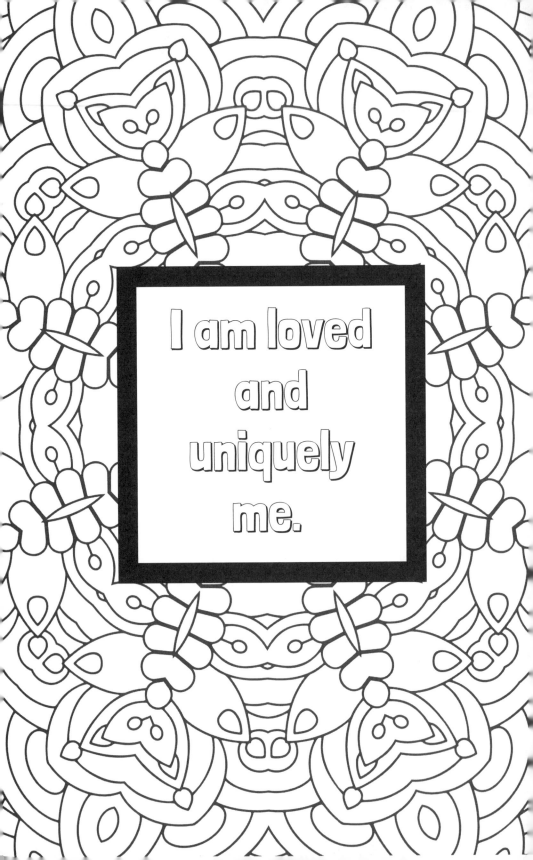

I am loved
and
uniquely
me.

Write about how this affirmation makes you feel. Or you can simply write it over and over again.

THIS WEEK

_____

Dates

3 Things I Have To Do:

1

2

3

2 Things I Am Looking Forward To:

1

2

1 Habit I Will Practice:

Color or mark the days you practice this habit. Write notes about how it feels to complete it or any challenges you face.

Take a break from drinking sugary, sweet drinks such as soft drinks/sodas and fruit juices for a week.

M T W T F S S

What's your favorite spot to hangout in at home? At school? Describe the space and the things that make it so comfortable. How does it feel? What does it smell like?

CONFIDENCE CHECK-IN

How are you doing? Write or draw whatever is on your mind or heart.

THIS WEEK

_____
Dates

3 Things I Have To Do:

1

2

3

2 Things I Am Looking Forward To:

1

2

1 Habit I Will Practice:

Color or mark the days you practice this habit. Write notes about how it feels to complete it or any challenges you face.

Go jogging for 10 minutes each day.

| M | T | W | T | F | S | S |

Congratulations! You've just won one million dollars. What would you spend your money on first? Would you give any of it away?

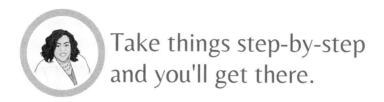

Take things step-by-step
and you'll get there.

THIS WEEK

_____

Dates

3 Things I Have To Do:

1

2

3

2 Things I Am Looking Forward To:

1

2

1 Habit I Will Practice:

Color or mark the days you practice this habit. Write notes about how it feels to complete it or any challenges you face.

Sing one of your favorite songs in the shower/bathroom.

| M | T | W | T | F | S | S |

Which subject do you hope you never have to deal with again in life? Which subject could you take all day? Why?

CONFIDENCE CHECK-IN
How are you doing? Write or draw whatever is on your mind or heart.

THIS WEEK

_____

Dates

3 Things I Have To Do:

1

2

3

2 Things I Am Looking Forward To:

1

2

1 Habit I Will Practice:

Color or mark the days you practice this habit. Write notes about how it feels to complete it or any challenges you face.

Make up your bed every day.

What are three things you can do to relieve your stress? Draw a picture of your face, smiling and relaxed.

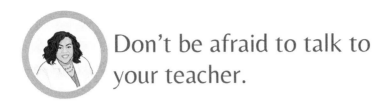

Don't be afraid to talk to your teacher.

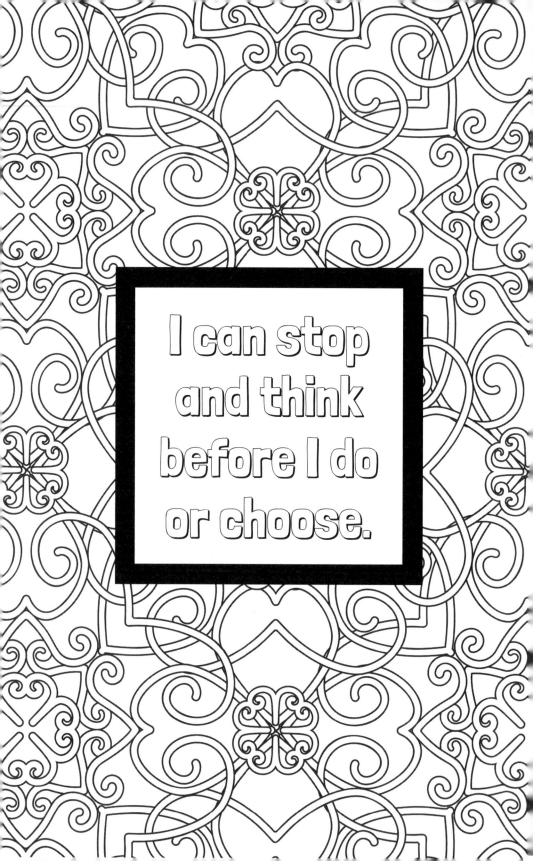

I can stop
and think
before I do
or choose.

Write about how this affirmation makes you feel. Or you can simply write it over and over again.

THIS WEEK

_____

Dates

3 Things I Have To Do:

1

2

3

2 Things I Am Looking Forward To:

1

2

1 Habit I Will Practice:

Color or mark the days you practice this habit. Write notes about how it feels to complete it or any challenges you face.

Pull out an old book and reread it, making note of anything you missed the first time.

| M | T | W | T | F | S | S |

What are three questions you wish adults would stop asking you? What are three questions you wish you could ask adults?

CONFIDENCE CHECK-IN
How are you doing? Write or draw whatever is on your mind or heart.

THIS WEEK

_____

Dates

3 Things I Have To Do:

1

2

3

2 Things I Am Looking Forward To:

1

2

1 Habit I Will Practice:

Color or mark the days you practice this habit. Write notes about how it feels to complete it or any challenges you face.

Tell a silly joke every day.

M	T	W	T	F	S	S

When you get really upset or angry, is there something or someone that calms you down? Describe what calm feels like — in your heart, your fingertips, and your mind.

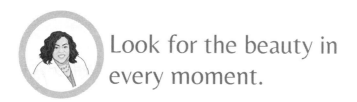

Look for the beauty in every moment.

THIS WEEK

_____

Dates

3 Things I Have To Do:

1

2

3

2 Things I Am Looking Forward To:

1

2

1 Habit I Will Practice:

Color or mark the days you practice this habit. Write notes about how it feels to complete it or any challenges you face.

Say thank you to adults who help you throughout this week.

| M | T | W | T | F | S | S |

What piece of advice has a family member, mentor, or teacher shared with you that has really helped you? Have you thanked them for it?

CONFIDENCE CHECK-IN
How are you doing? Write or draw whatever is on your mind or heart.

THIS WEEK

_____
Dates

3 Things I Have To Do:

1

2

3

2 Things I Am Looking Forward To:

1

2

1 Habit I Will Practice:

Color or mark the days you practice this habit. Write notes about how it feels to complete it or any challenges you face.

Write notes to family members sharing three reasons you love and appreciate them.

M T W T F S S

Think back to a time when you gave your best to a project or something important to you. Describe what that experience was like. What made you most proud?

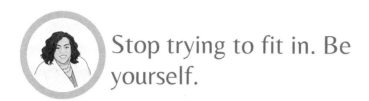

Stop trying to fit in. Be yourself.

I will encourage myself to succeed.

Write about how this affirmation makes you feel. Or you can simply write it over and over again.

THIS WEEK

_____

Dates

3 Things I Have To Do:

1

2

3

2 Things I Am Looking Forward To:

1

2

1 Habit I Will Practice:

Color or mark the days you practice this habit. Write notes about how it feels to complete it or any challenges you face.

Learn a dance that was popular years before you were born.

What's the craziest thing that's happened to you personally this year?
What's the craziest thing that's happened at your school?

CONFIDENCE CHECK-IN
How are you doing? Write or draw whatever is on your mind or heart.

THIS WEEK

_____ Dates

3 Things I Have To Do:

1

2

3

2 Things I Am Looking Forward To:

1

2

1 Habit I Will Practice:

Color or mark the days you practice this habit. Write notes about how it feels to complete it or any challenges you face.

Think of something extra kind you can do for someone else each day.

| M | T | W | T | F | S | S |

Imagine you're at your graduation ceremony and you have to speak. The principal asked you to share some words of wisdom with the freshmen class. What would you say?

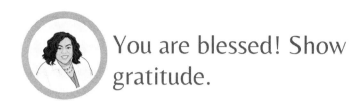

You are blessed! Show gratitude.

THIS WEEK

_____
Dates

3 Things I Have To Do:

1

2

3

2 Things I Am Looking Forward To:

1

2

1 Habit I Will Practice:

Color or mark the days you practice this habit. Write notes about how it feels to complete it or any challenges you face.

Read about people from your state and/or city who accomplished great things.

M T W T F S S

Has someone ever been dishonest with you? How did you find out they were lying? What did you do?

CONFIDENCE CHECK-IN
How are you doing? Write or draw whatever is on your mind or heart.

THIS WEEK

_____
Dates

3 Things I Have To Do:

1

2

3

2 Things I Am Looking Forward To:

1

2

1 Habit I Will Practice:

Color or mark the days you practice this habit. Write notes about how it feels to complete it or any challenges you face.

Sort through your own dirty laundry this week. If you don't know how to, ask.

| M | T | W | T | F | S | S |

You've been invited to be interviewed on television as a representative of all teens. What would you say are the top three issues/problems teens care most about right now? How would you fix them?

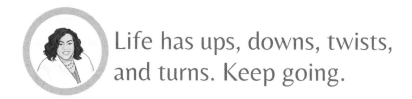

Life has ups, downs, twists,
and turns. Keep going.

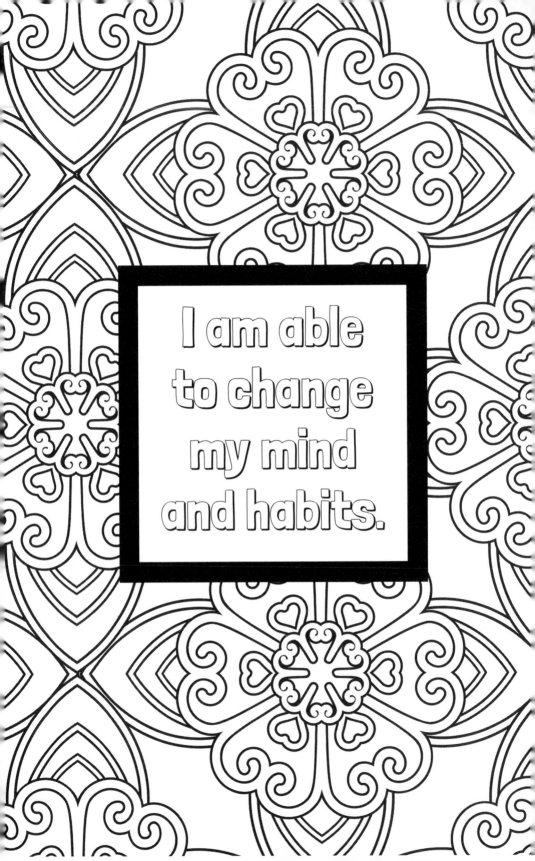

I am able
to change
my mind
and habits.

Write about how this affirmation makes you feel. Or you can simply write it over and over again.

THIS WEEK

_____

Dates

3 Things I Have To Do:

1

2

3

2 Things I Am Looking Forward To:

1

2

1 Habit I Will Practice:

Color or mark the days you practice this habit. Write notes about how it feels to complete it or any challenges you face.

Do not eat any chips, cookies, or candy this week.

M T W T F S S

Think of something you see people doing or saying that you believe is wrong, unhealthy, or unkind. Why do you believe it's 'wrong?' In your opinion, what's a better way?

CONFIDENCE CHECK-IN

How are you doing? Write or draw whatever is on your mind or heart.

THIS WEEK

_____

Dates

3 Things I Have To Do:

1

2

3

2 Things I Am Looking Forward To:

1

2

1 Habit I Will Practice:

Color or mark the days you practice this habit. Write notes about how it feels to complete it or any challenges you face.

Put away your tablet/phone or anything with a screen during every mealtime this week.

M T W T F S S

What *don't* you want to be when you grow up? List three characteristics of people or professions you *do not* want to be anything like as an adult.

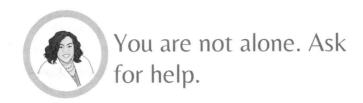

You are not alone. Ask for help.

THIS WEEK

_____

Dates

3 Things I Have To Do:

❶

❷

❸

2 Things I Am Looking Forward To:

❶

❷

1 Habit I Will Practice:

Color or mark the days you practice this habit. Write notes about how it feels to complete it or any challenges you face.

Watch your favorite movie and episodes of your favorite TV show from childhood.

M T W T F S S

Has a teacher or adult disappointed you in the past? What happened? What's one thing you learned from that experience?

CONFIDENCE CHECK-IN
How are you doing? Write or draw whatever is on your mind or heart.

THIS WEEK

_____

Dates

3 Things I Have To Do:

1

2

3

2 Things I Am Looking Forward To:

1

2

1 Habit I Will Practice:

Color or mark the days you practice this habit. Write notes about how it feels to complete it or any challenges you face.

Ask your parent, grandparent, guardian, or sibling to tell you about when they were in the same grade as you.

| M | T | W | T | F | S | S |

It's been declared that after some science experiment, you are now a superhero. What are your superpowers and what crime would you fight first?

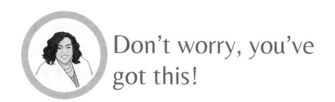

Don't worry, you've got this!

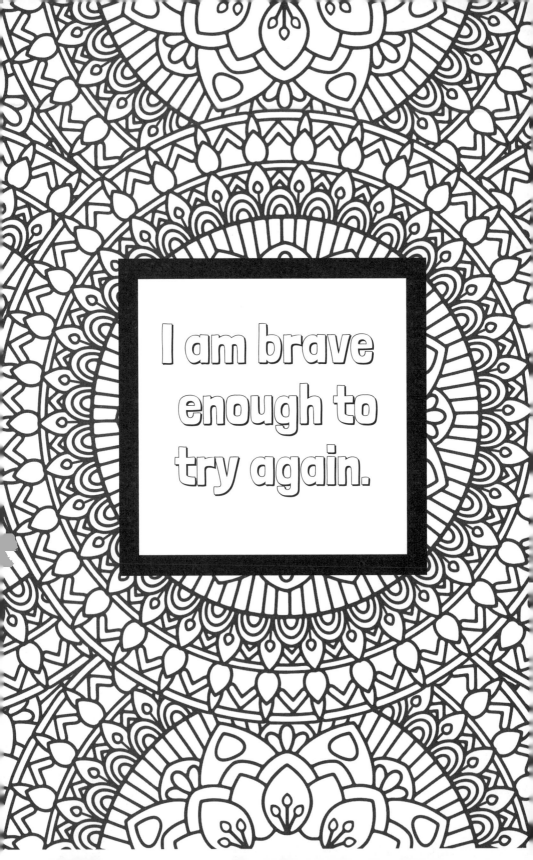

Write about how this affirmation makes you feel. Or you can simply write it over and over again.

THIS WEEK

_____
Dates

3 Things I Have To Do:

1

2

3

2 Things I Am Looking Forward To:

1

2

1 Habit I Will Practice:

Color or mark the days you practice this habit. Write notes about how it feels to complete it or any challenges you face.

Take a moment to notice the nature around you – trees, plants or flowers, color of the sky, sounds, etc. Find one beautiful thing each day.

M T W T F S S

What are three things you don't feel comfortable sharing with friends? What is keeping you from talking about it with them? How does it feel to hold it in?

CONFIDENCE CHECK-IN
How are you doing? Write or draw whatever is on your mind or heart.

THIS WEEK

_____

Dates

3 Things I Have To Do:

1

2

3

2 Things I Am Looking Forward To:

1

2

1 Habit I Will Practice:

Color or mark the days you practice this habit. Write notes about how it feels to complete it or any challenges you face.

Learn how to say hello and goodbye in a different language. Teach it to someone else.

What extracurricular or afterschool activity is your favorite? Why do you enjoy it so much?

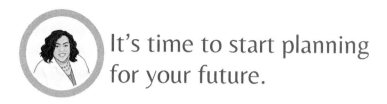

It's time to start planning for your future.

THIS WEEK

_____

Dates

3 Things I Have To Do:

1

2

3

2 Things I Am Looking Forward To:

1

2

1 Habit I Will Practice:

Color or mark the days you practice this habit. Write notes about how it feels to complete it or any challenges you face.

Write a letter to yourself, sharing the top things you love about yourself.

What skill or activity do you enjoy that you wish you had more time or help to learn how to get better? Are there things you can do to improve?

CONFIDENCE CHECK-IN
How are you doing? Write or draw whatever is on your mind or heart.

THIS WEEK

_____
Dates

3 Things I Have To Do:

1

2

3

2 Things I Am Looking Forward To:

1

2

1 Habit I Will Practice:

Color or mark the days you practice this habit. Write notes about how it feels to complete it or any challenges you face.

Show up or be prepared 15 minutes early for every appointment this week.

M T W T F S S

If you could achieve anything you wanted in life after high school, what would it be? Draw an example of what it would look like to accomplish this goal.

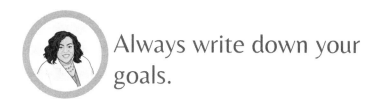

Always write down your goals.

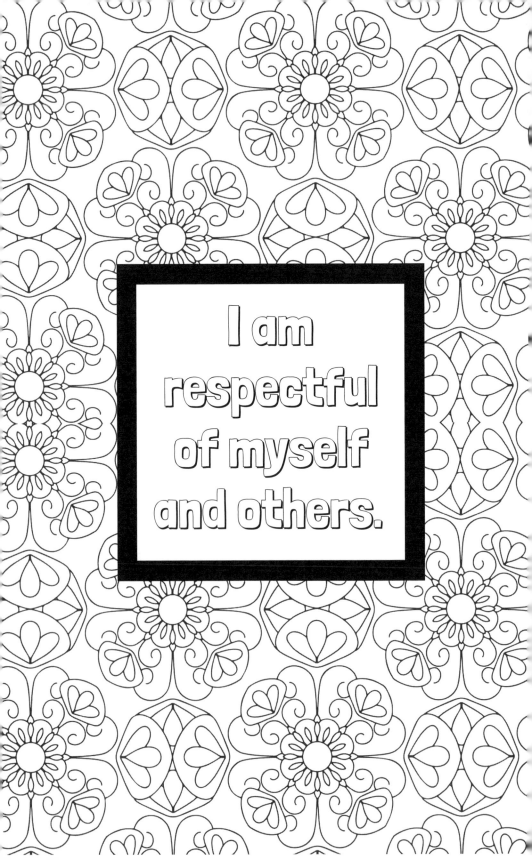

I am
respectful
of myself
and others.

Write about how this affirmation makes you feel. Or you can simply write it over and over again.

THIS WEEK

_____

Dates

3 Things I Have To Do:

1

2

3

2 Things I Am Looking Forward To:

1

2

1 Habit I Will Practice:

Color or mark the days you practice this habit. Write notes about how it feels to complete it or any challenges you face.

Learn the lyrics to a new song.

M T W T F S S

When's the last time someone said 'no' or disappointed you? What did they do and how did you respond?

CONFIDENCE CHECK-IN

How are you doing? Write or draw whatever is on your mind or heart.

THIS WEEK

_____
Dates

3 Things I Have To Do:

1

2

3

2 Things I Am Looking Forward To:

1

2

1 Habit I Will Practice:

Color or mark the days you practice this habit. Write notes about how it feels to complete it or any challenges you face.

Compliment classmates who are really good at a particular subject or activity.

What are five things you want to see happen in the next five years with you or your friends or family?

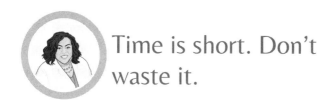

Time is short. Don't waste it.

THIS WEEK

_____
Dates

3 Things I Have To Do:

1

2

3

2 Things I Am Looking Forward To:

1

2

1 Habit I Will Practice:

Color or mark the days you practice this habit. Write notes about how it feels to complete it or any challenges you face.

Watch the sunrise and sunset this week.

M T W T F S S

Is there a book, show, or movie that you enjoy so much you wish you could visit? Imagine what would happen if you were a character in the story. Who would you be and why?

CONFIDENCE CHECK-IN

How are you doing? Write or draw whatever is on your mind or heart.

THIS WEEK

_____

Dates

3 Things I Have To Do:

1

2

3

2 Things I Am Looking Forward To:

1

2

1 Habit I Will Practice:

Color or mark the days you practice this habit. Write notes about how it feels to complete it or any challenges you face.

Check-in with your teachers and school guidance counselor to see if there's anything you should be doing that will help you achieve your academic goals.

Do you sometimes worry about being or looking perfect? Who or what makes you believe you have to be perfect?

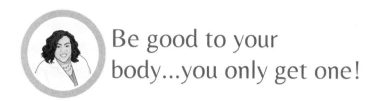

Be good to your
body...you only get one!

I can ask
for help to
learn a
better way.

Write about how this affirmation makes you feel. Or you can simply write it over and over again.

THIS WEEK

_____

Dates

3 Things I Have To Do:

1

2

3

2 Things I Am Looking Forward To:

1

2

1 Habit I Will Practice:

Color or mark the days you practice this habit. Write notes about how it feels to complete it or any challenges you face.

Keep your room extra neat and tidy without an adult having to tell you to do so.

What has surprised you most about school? If you were in charge what would you change? What would you keep?

CONFIDENCE CHECK-IN
How are you doing? Write or draw whatever is on your mind or heart.

THIS WEEK

_____

Dates

3 Things I Have To Do:

1

2 `

3

2 Things I Am Looking Forward To:

1

2

1 Habit I Will Practice:

Color or mark the days you practice this habit. Write notes about how it feels to complete it or any challenges you face.

**Mention to your parent, guardian, teacher, or coach something
that you're having trouble figuring out on your own.**

| M | T | W | T | F | S | S |

What's a habit you do that others may find funny or interesting? What made you start doing it?

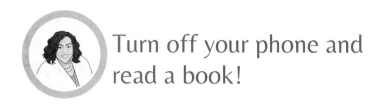

Turn off your phone and read a book!

THIS WEEK

_____

Dates

3 Things I Have To Do:

1

2

3

2 Things I Am Looking Forward To:

1

2

1 Habit I Will Practice:

Color or mark the days you practice this habit. Write notes about how it feels to complete it or any challenges you face.

Go to bed 20 minutes earlier every night.

M T W T F S S

Is it hard for you to share your thoughts and feelings with others? Why or why not?

CONFIDENCE CHECK-IN
How are you doing? Write or draw whatever is on your mind or heart.

THIS WEEK

_____
Dates

3 Things I Have To Do:

1

2

3

2 Things I Am Looking Forward To:

1

2

1 Habit I Will Practice:

Color or mark the days you practice this habit. Write notes about how it feels to complete it or any challenges you face.

Talk to your parents/grandparents or guardian about one of the goals you have for this week. Share a goal you have for next year.

What is something that adults say all the time but it makes no sense to you? How do you wish you could correct them?

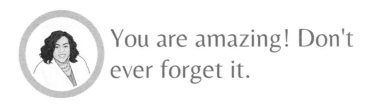

You are amazing! Don't ever forget it.

I can get through tough times.

Write about how this affirmation makes you feel. Or you can simply write it over and over again.

THIS WEEK

_____

Dates

3 Things I Have To Do:

1

2

3

2 Things I Am Looking Forward To:

1

2

1 Habit I Will Practice:

Color or mark the days you practice this habit. Write notes about how it feels to complete it or any challenges you face.

Measure out or only eat a serving size (based on the nutritional label) for every snack you enjoy this week.

| M | T | W | T | F | S | S |

What would your day look like if you could control your schedule? What time would you get up? What would you do? Where would you go?

CONFIDENCE CHECK-IN

How are you doing? Write or draw whatever is on your mind or heart.

THIS WEEK

_____
Dates

3 Things I Have To Do:

1

2

3

2 Things I Am Looking Forward To:

1

2

1 Habit I Will Practice:

Color or mark the days you practice this habit. Write notes about how it feels to complete it or any challenges you face.

Do jumping jacks for at least five minutes every day.

What's something good and nice that you do that no one seems to notice? How can you reward yourself?

Be as beautiful on the inside
as you are on the outside.

 **THIS WEEK**

_____

Dates

3 Things I Have To Do:

1

2

3

2 Things I Am Looking Forward To:

1

2

1 Habit I Will Practice:

Color or mark the days you practice this habit. Write notes about how it feels to complete it or any challenges you face.

Memorize an inspirational poem.

| M | T | W | T | F | S | S |

Imagine a close friend or family member is going through a problem and they're ready to give up. Write an encouraging note to them.

CONFIDENCE CHECK-IN

How are you doing? Write or draw whatever is on your mind or heart.

THIS WEEK

_____

Dates

3 Things I Have To Do:

1

2

3

2 Things I Am Looking Forward To:

1

2

1 Habit I Will Practice:

Color or mark the days you practice this habit. Write notes about how it feels to complete it or any challenges you face.

Call or talk to younger family members about their school life.

| M | T | W | T | F | S | S |

What has been your favorite hairstyle so far? Why? Doodle what it looks like.

It's important to be well-rounded.

_____
_____
_____
_____
_____
_____
_____
_____
_____
_____
_____
_____
_____
_____
_____
_____
_____
_____
_____
_____
_____
_____
_____
_____
_____
_____
_____
_____
_____
_____
_____

THIS WEEK

_____

Dates

3 Things I Have To Do:

1

2

3

2 Things I Am Looking Forward To:

1

2

1 Habit I Will Practice:

Color or mark the days you practice this habit. Write notes about how it feels to complete it or any challenges you face.

Share about problems you solved with your family and friends.

Outside of school, who teaches you the most? What lessons have you learned?

CONFIDENCE CHECK-IN

How are you doing? Write or draw whatever is on your mind or heart.

THIS WEEK

_____

Dates

3 Things I Have To Do:

1

2

3

2 Things I Am Looking Forward To:

1

2

1 Habit I Will Practice:

Color or mark the days you practice this habit. Write notes about how it feels to complete it or any challenges you face.

Play a game you used to play when you were younger with a family member or friend.

M T W T F S S

What scares you most about growing older? Have you ever shared this with anyone? Why or why not?

Treat everybody right.

THIS WEEK

_____

Dates

3 Things I Have To Do:

1

2

3

2 Things I Am Looking Forward To:

1

2

1 Habit I Will Practice:

Color or mark the days you practice this habit. Write notes about how it feels to complete it or any challenges you face.

Organize your room, get rid of any clutter or donate old items you no longer use.

| M | T | W | T | F | S | S |

Think about a time when someone you know made a mistake. Did they correct it? What do you wish you could have told them to do differently?

CONFIDENCE CHECK-IN
How are you doing? Write or draw whatever is on your mind or heart.

THIS WEEK

_____

Dates

3 Things I Have To Do:

1

2

3

2 Things I Am Looking Forward To:

1

2

1 Habit I Will Practice:

Color or mark the days you practice this habit. Write notes about how it feels to complete it or any challenges you face.

Review all of your "weeks" and entries in this journal and note changes you've made and habits you kept.

Get really quiet and notice your senses. Write down one thing you smell, two things you hear, and three things you feel. Now draw or doodle an object that you see in the room with you.

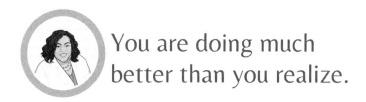

You are doing much
better than you realize.

NOTE TO SELF

NOTE TO SELF

NOTE TO SELF

NOTE TO SELF

MEET DR. CECE

Dr. Charnetta Colton-Poole (a.k.a. Dr. CeCe) is a Board-certified Pediatrician, medical copywriter and communication strategist, speaker, and writer. A true Georgia peach, Dr. Charnetta received her Bachelor of Science degree from the University of Georgia and her Master of Science degree from Georgia State University. She received her Doctor of Medicine degree from Morehouse School of Medicine and completed her Pediatric and Adolescent Medicine Residency at Emory University School of Medicine in Atlanta, GA. Dr. Charnetta has over 25 years experience in the writing field and is the Amazon #1 Best-Selling Author of 'The 10 Commandments of Communication for Doctors'. She is also a Christian playwright with multiple writing and directing credits to her name. Dr. Charnetta is a recipient of the University of Georgia Top 40 under 40 Alumni award and the Billie Wright Adams Excellence in Medicine award. She is also an active member of Alpha Kappa Alpha Sorority, Inc. She is a proud wife and mom and enjoys spending time with family, singing, and SEC Football. Write Through It is her first guided journal. She is currently working on a series of kids books and videos that will help kids of all ages better understand medical illness.